NOTES
for a Young Prince
By HSH Prince Alexi Lubomirski

Illustrated by Carlos Aponte
Designed by Edna Isabel Acosta
Edited by Evelyn Otero Figueroa

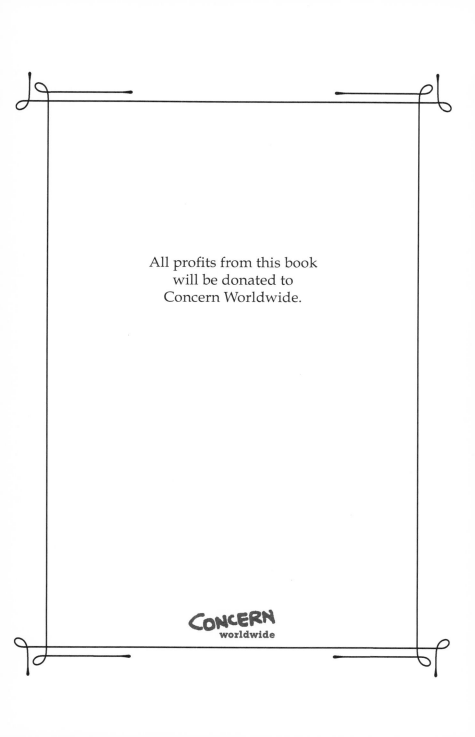

All profits from this book
will be donated to
Concern Worldwide.

Author: Alexi Lubomirski

Illustration: Carlos Aponte

Design: Edna Isabel Acosta

Edition: Evelyn Otero Figueroa

Print: CreateSpace, Inc.

ISBN 978-0615932606

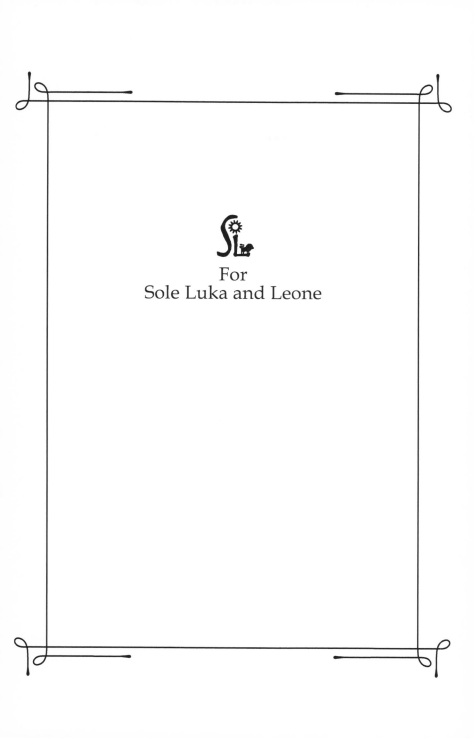

For
Sole Luka and Leone

YOU ARE MY SONS, BORN OF LOVE.

I see in your eyes all the nations and
bloods that comprise you,
drawing from many soils, lands, and coasts.
In you, lies the very best of me;
all that is good that I have to offer.

Cradling you in my arms,
I gaze upon a life yet unknown.
Stand then, on my shoulders
and scale the heavens!
Take from me all that is honorable,
all that is noble and true,
leaving behind any malice or malcontent.

Watching you grow is life's single greatest pleasure.
Each new step, each new word, lifts my heart and
brings light into my world.
May God give me the courage needed to release you
from my arms, safe in the knowledge that I have
guided you fair and true.

Let my arms grant you protection.
Let my love teach you compassion.
Let my actions guide your character.
Let my words give you wisdom.

YOU ARE LOVE. YOU ARE LOVED. YOU ARE MY SONS.

— Alexi Lubomirski

MY HUMBLE THANKS GO TO

John Mainwaring,
Pamela Mainwaring,
HSH Prince Ladislas Lubomirski,
HSH Princess Giada Lubomirska,
Michael Mainwaring,
Nick Mainwaring,
Vituca Beardsell,
Edna Isabel Acosta,
Evelyn Otero Figueroa,
and Carlos Aponte.

INTRODUCTION

I was born to a Peruvian/English mother and a Polish/French father in London, England.

My childhood was spent between England and Botswana with my mother and English stepfather. At the age of eleven, I was informed of my father's and therefore my title. The title of prince.

It was a title that stretched back over half a millennium. Yet after two world wars and the rise of communism had lost centuries of art, land, palaces, and family treasures. It was a title with no material evidence but a wealth of history.

So what is this title's meaning now? How was I to wear this royal badge? As the sole male heir of my family's line, how was I to fulfill my duty to honor my ancestors' accomplishments and carry this title for my descendents.

"It is in you," my mother told me. "If you are to be a prince in today's world, you have to be a prince in your heart and in your actions."

Now I have two sons. When I tell them of their title, what relevance will it hold for them today?

How should they carry this banner? There are no lands to conquer, no borders to protect, and no treasures to manage. Their wealth lies in their actions, and their legacy will be the manner in which they choose to live their lives.

DEAR SONS . . . .

• • • • • Be CHIVALROUS at all times.
Stand up
when introduced to women.
Open doors for them,
help carry their belongings,
and protect them from harm.

Create your own KINGDOM and empire.
You may be born into palaces
or born on the street,
but it is up to you
to create your own life.

Nurture your SPIRITUALITY.
        Know that you are joined
        to everything in this world
        by one force and one energy.
        Treat everything in this planet
        as you would want to be treated.

Know that every word
that leaves your mouth
can never be taken back.
Let every word be positive
and used for good.
Negative words lead
to negative energy.
Speak positively
and allow POSITIVE ENERGY to flow.

Your most POWERFUL weapon is your smile.
Use it to
shed light
onto any situation.

COMMON COURTESY:
"Please" and
"thank you"
can never be overused.

Treat everyone with RESPECT,
from the richest
to the poorest person
on the street.

PROTECT the earth and the environment
        as if it was
        your own home
        or family member.
        It looks after you too.

Be generous with praise, ENCOURAGEMENT,
and compliments.
It is important
for people to know
when they have done
a good job or deed.

When you feel down, SMILE.
Your mind and body
will follow suit.

Speak LANGUAGES.
Each language is a gift
and a key that opens up
hundreds of new doors.

Be a "CITIZEN OF THE WORLD"
rather than just one country.
Travel the world, and see other cultures
and places. See the different way
people live and treat each other.
By doing this you will open up
your mind and broaden your horizons.

Live LIFE to the fullest every day.
Approach everything
with an open mind
and positive energy.

When making a toast,
make it to something rather
than just saying "CHEERS."

When possible,
take care of the bill
when DINING with a woman.

BALANCE is the greatest gift
you can give yourself.
Know that to succeed in life
and to be truly "rich"
you must be successful
in all areas of work, love,
and family at the same time.

Nurture your CREATIVITY.
          Paint, write, sing, and play music.
          All these are forms of expression
          that can help center and align
          your thoughts and
          help you find balance.

Be a PASSIONATE friend.

Be a devoted FAMILY member.
Look after them.
They are one of the few
constants in your life.

Stay HEALTHY.
If your body is fit, so is your mind.

Your HISTORY can be an excuse to fail
or a reason to succeed. You decide.

When shaking hands, be firm
but not to the point of squeezing
the hand into submission.
It should show CONFIDENCE,
not competitiveness.

Be generous with your WEALTH.
Remember that there is
a flow of money,
and you have to give
so that you can receive.

Be UNDERSTANDING to other people. Always try to comprehend the reasons for their actions before you rush to judge.

Open your eyes to all the BEAUTY,
magic, and miracles in this world.
The more you open your mind to them,
the more they will become apparent.

Learn to LISTEN.

       You will learn more in one minute
       of someone else speaking,
       rather than listening to yourself
       speak for an hour.

Know your own WORTH and trust your heart.
One day someone
can shower you with flattery,
and the next day
the same person can curse you.
You cannot let the flattery
or curse affect you.
Know why you do things,
trust your heart,
and always do your best.
Only you can judge
your true worth.

Have confidence in your abilities.
It is natural to feel fear, but have COURAGE,
be confident, push forward,
and your fear
will gradually disappear.

Embrace the fact
that you are different
to other people.
Being different
sets you apart
from the rest
and will allow you to SHINE.

PROTECT those weaker than yourself.
One day you may also need help
from someone stronger.

Be AMBITIOUS!
    Know in your heart that you can
    achieve anything you put your mind to.
    Set yourself ambitious goals and
    work your hardest towards them,
    even if they seem unreachable.
    The universe will help you
    along the way.

Take RESPONSIBILITY for your actions.
When you succeed, be happy and
share your joy with others.
When you fail, blame no one else.

Always try to see the POSITIVE in people
and circumstances.
If you do this,
your life will be positive.

Be open to new EXPERIENCES,
new people, and new lands.
Scare yourself a little bit every day
by taking advantage of every
scenario that life puts in front
of you. Speak up. Take the leap!

The sooner you realize
that coincidences do not exist,
the sooner you will be able
to recognize the SIGNS
that life gives you.

LAUGH out loud every day!

Remember to stay CHILDLIKE.
>   Never take life too seriously.
>   Life is a beautiful present
>   and should be treated as such.
>   A gift of joy to you and
>   those around you.

Remember that your
GUARDIANS and ANCESTORS
are with you always.
Ready to hear your prayers
when you need their help,
and eager to celebrate with you
when you are happy.

Be GRATEFUL every morning when you
    wake up and every night before bed.
    Be thankful for having legs that help you run,
    for arms that allow you to hug,
    for eyes that let you see the sun,
    for ears that let you hear your loved ones voices,
    for skin that lets you feel your mother's kiss…
    Grateful for all the blessings and opportunities
    that you are given every day.

Be RESPECTFUL to women.

Make the most of every OPPORTUNITY
that is given to you,
as they are gifts
from the universe
to help you reach
your goals.

SAVOR this world's delights.
The world has millions of flavors,
foods, views, tastes, and sounds.
Savor them all!

Be SENSITIVE to people around you.
Take into account
how your actions
can affect others and
be respectful of them.

Learn other people's CULTURES,
and respect their beliefs and wishes.

PRAY. Whether in a church, a field,
        on a mountaintop, walking to school
        or in your bedroom, pray.
        Have conversations with God,
        the universe, your ancestors or guardians.
        Thank them for all that you have
        and for the promise of what is to come.
        Ask them for help and guidance.
        They will always be there for you.
        The more you talk to each other,
        the better they will know you
        and be able to help you.

Try to do at least one GOOD DEED every day.
It will soon become a habit
and you will become
a better person
for it.

Your POSTURE can define your mood.
Sit up straight and strong.
This will allow energy
to flow more freely
in your body.

Being "right" is not always
what is best for the situation.
Knowing which BATTLES to fight
and which ones to leave
is a powerful lesson.

HELP others achieve their goals.
It is just as important to help others,
as it is to help yourself.

Today may be easy.
Tomorrow may be difficult.
Remember that you were born
with every skill you need
to ride each wave.
Stay loose and calm, and you can ADAPT
to any situation easily.

Do a job that you are
passionate about.
If you are blessed
to have a hobby as a job,
you never have to WORK
a day in your life.

LEADERSHIP. Lead by example.
Be the best you can be, and others
will be inspired to do the same.

Be PREPARED. Every situation can be researched and planned for. Being knowledgeable beforehand will allow you to be ready for any opportunity that presents itself.

Accept the EVOLUTION of land,
property, and money.
These things can come and
go quickly, but your spirit
and soul are yours forever.

Show appreciation for your blessings in life by blessing others with gifts of kindness. Give 10% of your profits to CHARITY, family members or friends in need. Hoarding your wealth causes the flow of money to go stale. Keep the cycle moving so that you maintain the flow of blessings.

LOVE. Love with all your heart.
It may be broken from time to time,
but only so that it can prepare
for your one true love.

Be ROMANTIC. Think of different ways
    each day to express your love
    to your loved ones.
    Love needs to be encouraged,
    fed, and celebrated.
    Do it it every day!

Listen to your HEART!
It is your greatest guide and advisor.
The more you listen to it,
the stronger it will become and
you will always make
the best decisions.

When dining with a woman,
give her the seat facing out
with a view of the restaurant,
whilst you take the seat facing in.
She will be free to enjoy the view
and the people, but your
ATTENTION will be on her and her alone.

BREATHE. Whenever you are worried,
tired, upset or angry, breathe.
By breathing deeply you reopen
the flow in your body and balance
yourself. You will then be able
to see things clearly.

Let everything on Heaven
and Earth know when you are HAPPY
by screaming, shouting, laughing,
smiling, or singing. Your joy will
bring light to others.

Be HONORABLE in your dealings.
Do not try to cheat others
out of what they truly deserve
for your own benefit.

When you are tired,
double your efforts.
Take a shower, shave,
and put on clean clothes.
Your body and mind will feel ENERGIZED.

Be LOYAL to family,
friends, and loved ones.
Look after them
and they will look after you.
Maintain the flow of loyalty.

When you walk, WALK TALL.
Breathe deeply. Feel your chest
expand and smile with your whole
body at the blessings of life.
Let people see a proud, confident,
strong, and happy spirit.

Look after your TEETH.
They are the first thing
that people see when you smile!

Be HUMBLE. Let your actions
speak for themselves.
There is no need to shout
about your talents or achievements.

Accept the past and BELIEVE in the future.

Don't be lazy with your VOCABULARY. For example, instead of describing something as "nice," use one of the hundreds of other more descriptive adjectives to express your point.

LADIES first.

When meeting a woman,
always arrive early so that
she is not left WAITING.

Treat your BODY well.
You do not have a backup
in case you ruin it.

Be PROUD of your family's achievements
and history. You are the latest in a long line,
and should feel proud to be to be part
of that lineage. Make them proud of you
by forging ahead in your own manner.
Also by succeeding in family, happiness,
and spiritual evolution.

Do not toy with people's EMOTIONS.

Everyone who has achieved
something in this world
        has pearls of WISDOM
that you can learn from.
Model yourself on those
you admire. Ask questions.

Learn to cook.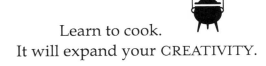
It will expand your CREATIVITY.

RESPECT your elders.
    Remember that they have been
    through all the stages of life
    that you still have yet to visit.
    They have many lessons for you.
    Be patient when they give you advice.

Manners make the MAN.

Listen to classical MUSIC.

It will create a peaceful ambience and inspire your creativity.

JUDGE people by their actions,
not by their skin color,
age or nationality.

When someone comes to you for advice, LISTEN.
Ask them how they feel
about the subject.
Often people have it in them
to solve their own problems,
they just need a sounding board
to help themselves.

Stay CALM.
    In arguments and discussions,
    think before you speak.
    Unnecessary things being said
    in the heat of the moment
    worsen fights.

First impressions do count.
Always introduce yourself the way
you want to be remembered.
Appearance is not everything,
but it is important to look your best
so that your inside and outside
both SHINE equally.

Be POLITE.
A little politeness goes a long way.

Walking down the street with a woman,
walk on the street side of her.
By doing this, you can SHIELD
her from any puddle that
a passing car may drive through.

Do not worry about making mistakes in life, as long as you LEARN from them.

Actively look for ways
to help people every day.
Be ALERT to your surroundings,
and be ready to jump into action
at a moment's notice.

Do not gossip.
It is nonproductive.
Keep your SPEECH and attitude positive.

Whenever possible,
dive into the sea,
even if only for a second.
It will INVIGORATE you.

Learn how to COMMUNICATE
clearly and calmly.
Communicate your feelings,
problems, and wishes.
Breathe, then communicate.

Keep a journal.
Apart from your memories,
write down your THOUGHTS.
This will help you
understand them better and
make room for new thoughts.

Be a people watcher.
Study people and how they INTERACT.
See how their actions affect
others around them.
This will help you get
the most out of dealing with
people in a friendly manner.

SAVE money.
Make sure you always have
more than you think you need,
in case any emergency
or surprise emerges.

Always remember
to write a THANK YOU note,
email or letter
as soon as possible
after you receive
a gift or a favor.

When you think of what
to leave behind to your DESCENDANTS,
remember that love,
spiritual guidance, and
knowledge will serve them
better than material things.

If you take loans or incur debts, make paying them back a priority. Leaving them hanging over you can be a weight on your shoulders and slow down your personal GROWTH.

Be passionate about everything
you do. By doing this you will do
everything to the best of your ABILITIES.
The more effort you put into
something, the more you will get out
of it; whether it is related to your
relationships, your career
or your family.

Define yourself by your actions,
not by your family history
or connections. When you
have lived your life,
you will be most proud
of your personal ACHIEVEMENTS,
not the things that were
just handed to you on a plate.

Make yourself HAPPY.
Invest in yourself by allowing
time for reading, sports, classes,
meditation, and leisure activities.
Do whatever makes you happy.
You must fuel your own light
if you are to be able
to share it with others.

Never take anything
for granted. What you
have today may be gone
tomorrow. Make the most
of each moment with
your friends, your family,
and your GOOD FORTUNE.

Be a BEACON of light to everything
you come into contact with.
Bring your light to people, places,
and things. When people leave
your company, let them leave
feeling better for having
run into you.

Have the courage to act.
Do not just learn these lessons,
put them into ACTION.

You do not need money,
palaces, land or treasures
to define you as a prince.
Be a prince in your own heart
and you will always be RICH.

If you do have a "PRINCELY DUTY"
it is only to be a good person,
kind, noble, and true. • • • • • • • • •

LOVE DADDY x

HSH PRINCE ALEXI LUBOMIRSKI was born to a Peruvian/English mother and a Polish/French father. He grew up between Botswana, Oxford, and London. At the age of eleven, he was informed of his true ancestral heritage and aristocratic bloodline.

Having not grown up in royal surroundings with all the trappings, he was the first of his family in 500 years to have the title with none of the material evidence.

Thanks to this displaced upbringing, and after much trial and error, he gradually succeeded in marrying his history with his present, managing to fulfill his role as the bearer of this title; and at the same time adapt the meaning in his modern day world.

Now, with two sons of his own, he lives a modern day life in New York, a city in the "New World." His duty being to pass down this title to his sons; and, at the same time, to adapt it so that it evolves with the times rather than become irrelevant and therefore extinct. Rather than focus on the past and what his family once had, he teaches his sons to forge ahead in a more spiritually aware manner and focus on what each of them believes the essence of their heritage means.

In his book, the word "prince" is used on one hand because of the family's title, and on the other because the word illustrates the "ideal" of a man that we should all strive to be.

Apart from being primarily a husband and a father, Alexi Lubomirski is a world-renowned fashion photographer.

www.alexilubomirski.com

Photo by Emily Jean Ullrich

CONTRIBUTORS

EDNA ISABEL ACOSTA
With a multidisciplinary vision, Edna Isabel Acosta has
worked as a creative director and designer in Puerto Rico.
Her creative portfolio includes over 20 years of continuous
work in the areas of branding, publications, museography,
silversmith, and jewelry design. Her work has been
awarded and exhibited in Puerto Rico, Europe, Latin
America, and USA.

www.behance.net/EdnaIsabelAcosta

EVELYN OTERO FIGUEROA
Studied economics and planning, but Evelyn Otero
Figueroa increasingly fell in love with the written word,
as she had before with statistics. Without abandoning her
technical background, journalism and editing invaded her
professional life. She pursued an ample career spectrum,
having worked in public service, consulting, banking,
newspapers, and magazines.

evelynoterofig@gmail.com

CARLOS APONTE
Fashion and general illustration, iconography, children
interactive stories, and comic strips are among the areas
that have successfully converged in Carlos Aponte's artistic
world. His experience and knowledge has led him to engage
in art education. For the past 15 years, Art Department
/New York, an international creative-talent agency, has
represented him.

www.carlosaponte.com

CONCERN
worldwide

Concern Worldwide is a non-governmental, international, humanitarian organization dedicated to the reduction of suffering and working towards the ultimate elimination of extreme poverty in the world's poorest countries.

Since its foundation in 1968, Concern Worldwide -through its work in emergencies and long-term development- has saved countless lives, relieved suffering, and provided opportunities for a better standard of living for millions of people. We work primarily in the countries ranked in the bottom 40 of the United Nations' Human Development Report. Concern implements emergency response programs as well as long-term development programs in the areas of livelihoods, health, HIV&AIDS, and education.

www.concernusa.org

Made in the USA
Charleston, SC
21 March 2014